Unveiling

A Metanoia Towards the Beauty of Truth

Ayushi Suman

BookLeaf Publishing

India | USA | UK

Editor approve the Content of this book published herein and do not make any representations or warranties of any kind, expressly of fitness for a particular purpose.

Made with ❤ on the BookLeaf Publishing Platform
www.bookleafpub.in
www.bookleafpub.com

To my mother, whose love and sensitivity nurtured my voice, encouraging me to express myself freely and discover beauty in life's small moments. To my father, patient listening and unwavering support made space for my creative musings and joyful explorations. To my brother, Ashu, whose boundless creativity and drive for innovation have always inspired me, and whose belief in my voice helped me overcome my doubts. And to my dearest college friend, Shreya, and my childhood best friend, Anshuya, whose optimism, strength, and courage illuminated my path when I needed it the most.

Acknowledgement

I wish to express my deepest gratitude to my family and friends for their unwavering support and encouragement. A special thanks to Abhishek, whose companionship during our countless walks along the college paths and his beautiful literary perspective on life helped me discover my poetic voice. His creative intellect and keen eye for detail, born from the natural poet within him, have been invaluable to me. I am profoundly grateful for his friendship and his steadfast belief in my work.

My sincere thanks also go to the wonderful people at BookLeaf Publishing for providing a platform to share my years of work and for their dedication to bringing this book to life.

And to you, dear readers, thank you for joining me on this journey through verse. I hope these poems resonate with you as deeply as they have with me.

Preface

This collection is a journey of self-reflection, capturing both fleeting moments and profound emotions. It spans the spectrum of feelings I have experienced and continue to do so— from the innocence of childhood to the complexities of becoming an emotionally attuned adult. Within these pages, you'll find expressions of gratitude and recognition for the people and experiences that have shaped my path and continue to inspire my growth. I invite you to uncover your own truths within these lines.

In the pages that follow, you will transverse the intricate landscapes of the human experience—a tapestry woven with threads of love, peace, war, and the quiet rebellion of the soul. These poems speak of the battles fought both outwardly and within, the delicate dance of hope and despair, and the profound moments that define who we are.

You will encounter verses echoing the sounds of societal protest, the whispers of introspection, and the gentle reminiscence of beautiful friendships. There are reflections of a world where madness takes its toll, but hope always rises to meet it. Through the verses, you will witness the resilience of the human spirit emerging—falling, yet rising again, like a flame rekindled in the darkest of the nights.

In the boundless imagination of a child, you may rediscover wonder; in the solemn reflections on war and peace, you may find a quiet yearning for a better tomorrow. This collection does not shy away from the complexities of our world but embraces them, offering solace, understanding, and a vision of what might be.

This book stands as a testament to the spectrum of emotions we all carry—pain, love, loss, and joy—and how every moment, whether marked by struggle or serenity, weaves the story of who we are. May these poems speak to your heart, stir something deep within, and remind you that we are all connected in our shared journey through the vast expanse of life.

Desolate Away!

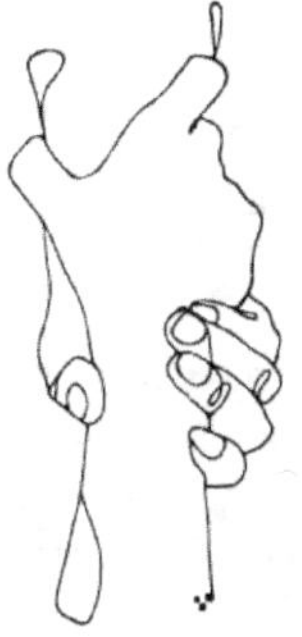

Under the bright and blazing sun,
I stood amidst the bracken-like,
Cage of the world,
With a boulder overheard,
Crushing me into ever smaller mounds.

With no mercy left,
Where no affection sat,
Only competition and jealousy dominated,
The hearts of the people,
As hateful havoc howling across the world.

In the middle of the ruthless war of ravens,
Reached a helping hand near me,
My brother's—

Like the flight of swallows from the heavens.
It was no less than a miracle,
But a favoured prodigy for me.

It wasn't just a help,
But a supplicate,
For me to fight my sullen nights fearlessly,
And percolate me,
Off my dreams, which came so drearily.

Now, I stand on the crest,
The desolation is away,
The sake of the help,
Or the stool where I stood so long,
Has disappeared gradually and added to my
capability
To stand on my own feet.

This indeed was an inadvertent help,
In my heart and memory,
It left a perennial impact.

And now that I suck the nectar of the sweet
flowers,
And not of sorrow,

Every day I wake up under the bask
And not under the horror!

Pretty as You Are

If pretty was all I wanted to show,
I'd simply walk in the crowd, aglow,
But your words obscure the woman into
which I'm grown,
It's not your shower of praise to which I bow,
But your sight where I'm a highbrow.

I wonder what hurts more:
Breaking that solemn vow,
Or the shattering of my desired bough?
To still keep my ground of being a proud
woman,
When in love,
Or to choose to make an exception,

And suit a paramour?

I doubt not an honorable man's love,
But does it have a price tag?

Not one, but many a beau did I lose,
For unlike many,
It wasn't for me a blinding love;
Ended in dismay,
Torn both into fragments ajar,
As that love wasn't so kind on my part!

I had all my heart to offer,
But was I to know
That all that roused you was
If I were to alter?
Did the marvelous woman in me disgust your
pride
So much as to drive you to spread around a
spiteful stride?

Determined to show me a woman's station,
I must say with a sigh,
"Yes, you won that day,
As at least I know that love

Isn't an excuse for a woman's feat to be side-lined!"

The Heart of Gaia

This weather makes me sad,
Happy, and relieved all at once.
I cry my heart out as it rains
Heavily outside, and muffling my cries.

The thunder is louder than my happiness,
And as mesmerizing as the sky is,
It's the scariest when it's fiddled with.
Just like the tempest within
This mind, body and soul.
I resonate, finally,
With the song of the rain and thunder.

It is Nature,
An embodiment of me,

And I cry,
I weep,
I wail,
For not a soul to hear,
But for that one lone fisherman caught in the
wrath of the sea.
He looks up at the sky,
And prays for mercy,
And she, the storm, mellows down for him,
Letting him cross the stormy waves,
Calming her grim.

Just as so,
Coddle me in your arms,
The way Mother Earth cradles,
Every drop of water from the rains,
And from there, sprouts the seed of life.

Nature is me.
I meld with the soil,
My soul is the air we breathe.
This petrifying calm
Still pacifies;
For it's this peace we came from,
And to it, we shall return.

I am the mother,
The Nature.
And she cries,
She weeps,
Before the calm,
She needs the embrace of love,
To keep her balance.

Shattered Resolve

I am scared to be sorry,
I am scared to be the way I am.
I never was this person,
Someone whom I've lost,
Someone whom I am tired of looking for.

The world has been brutal to me,
When I thought your heart was open to
shelter my fears.
I took my love and all my pride there to
reside.

Each day and every single night,
You fed me with your infatuated delights.
Little did I know,
I was just another bait for the raven,
Who never craved empathy,

But for whom all else was just another sloven.

I drowned into the depths of brevity,
Not knowing I was stepping into the well of
insanity,
Where nothing quenched my love but tears.

Love is a shackle,
Only edifies ways to rupture,
Human sentiments.
Lest it be a toy,
In the carefree hands of a wee boy,
It'd have split into
Pieces many,
Severed as broken shards of glass
That leave cracking slivers
Incurably bare forever.

I never showed such verbose ire
On another,
Until a mother's wisdom refined:
This world is no cakewalk,
For I came out with a gullible little heart.

You tricked me into your ways,

Now I walk strong
Yet with a feeble heart.
Now I laugh loud,
Having vehement wailing within.
Now I stay close,
Yet so far from the soul.
I portray myself as the daylight,
Yet in my heart,
The sun has forever set.
Lucky I have the moon by my side,
On each gloomy invasion,
The moonlight precipitates hope,
And whispers "You're alright!"
Kindles that love and warmth,
That the brute in you seized from my grip.
Your infestation ripped a part of me
Each time I tried to perceive affection
In all your darkness.

You have failed me,
And yes, I faltered in my ways.

And here I beg,
"Give me a hand,
Lift me from the wreck,

Teach me how to stand again,
Fill me with affection and the same innocence
again!"

Show me the light,
That glows from within!

Charm of Solace

One thing led to another,
But I wish to explore no further.
That solace in your aura, so serene,
Masks the flaming wounds to the soul that
still heals.

From walking past the patronizing boulevard,
Where my beauty was acutely scarred.
Through feuds & fight fluttering by my flaps,
And men parading their virile pride,
For women, then and now, are mere objects
to flaunt,
Clutched by their grip to daunt.

If romanticism was ever to be idealized,
It would be his soft embrace, gently devised.
You, my friend, have boldly confessed,
For the unspoken criminal inquest,
Committed by others under the male behest.

My admiration for your wiles
Is as cosmic as my abhorrence of those trivial smiles.
If only this mere jargon could contain your sanctity,
It shan't be in vanity,
For my regard for you surpasses every possibility!

Once, We Were!

From the brightest of my memories,
You'll be the first to come forth in hindsight,
To flicker away all the treacheries,
That put me through such an endless plight.

You remind me of the time when
Friendship was a token of love,
And I wonder if it's been that long since then,
That now it's all just a shove;
Disparate folks from the cluster,
Fighting and begging to care for the dove.

Even the thought of you
Begets a beam in my air.
For I owe it to you,
All the ardor that's added to my flair.

In our amble under the trees,
"A bed, a book and a room will do,"
You'd say, to make all of your dreams come
true.

You carry thy motions of mellowness;
You'd question *"Why do fireflies die?"*
And I marvel there,
Did I just stand under a downpour of luck
bestowed on me?
For I do not deserve to dwell around, a soul
so humble.
Or is it just how you are?

Pray, I may not often,
But how all the distress,
Shall escalate the realms wry,
If your benevolence were to prevail
Is all I think of now!

Selfless Embodiment

For humans, a fragrant flower,
A vessel filled with sweet nectar,
For the bees, the birds, it's enamour.
I bloom midst the thorns,
Yet people praise my bloom in a bridal
shower.
What irony I parade,
In my happy, jolly hour;
Lest someone knows my masquerade!

White as pure as driven snow,
With my shying shades of pale yellow,
Radiating from the centre,
Like the last ray of hope.

I bloom once,
Be it a peaceful night or a wretched sight;
I bloom no matter what is right.
For a man in search of warmth,
Shan't wait for the plight,
If only my act of flowering shall give him
respite.

Let my days of life be fleeting,
I shall, but,
Squeeze every drop of affection in my
beating;
With my each passing hour,
May might lie in parting all my greetings.
Mind not if I on occasion parade my pain,
In the course of my petals shedding,
And my sepals treading;
By looking old, torn and withered.

My demise shall make a bed of softened
petals,
Whereupon, young lovers dwell;
I fought no big battles,
Yet even my departure is divine.
I seek to spread no reign,

But to love and shine,
And all I ask for is,
Simply, allow me to prevail.

Loud Silence

Should I write?
Or should I think?
Should I sojourn in my past?
Or simply sink?
Though that absurd silence of vanity
Aims to kill me for no reason;
I yearned to live,
Unaware, what for,
No cause, though, even to die for.

I stayed...I sat... for hours,
Nothing did I expect,
But bowed to the candour of the moment;
Learning from every aspect;

Both of life and that of death.

And let the silence act upon me,
Then saw if it could flee,
From the ground it held too tight,
The ground for the righteous to thrive.

I was gripped by the mesmerizing instant,
When it uttered the shrillest cry, the loudest
voice,
Of the pettiest, most pitiable being,
The silence of the silence!

Only then did I grasp how thunderous one's
silence could be.
My ethics revived, sensations uproared,
I was taken aback.
For a while, I knew
How frivolous we had been with time,
How cruelly we handled the zest,
Learning what politics was *not* to teach!

Silence utters,
"When the sword's on your neck,
Do you then realize what hope tastes like?

And how bitter it is when it rots under the filth
Of phony parliamentary talks?
Now that you could taste it,
Would it not be the sweetest,
Even when it feels near hopeless? Yes?
No? Then how could you?
How could you even think of blemishing the
beacon of hope in a gullible being?
No amount of fights,
Nor any protests,
Have moved you—
But this Silence now is audible to you?
Then feel the sorrow, the anguish,
And endure it.
And yet persist dumb, of no worth!"

Was Silence choking me to death?
Or was this its plight?
It had no closure—
But this Silence in my
Introspection did teach me the lesson!

Darkness Thrives as Virtue Dies

Dark clouds don't foretell the dread of destruction,
But the victory of injustice over rightful induction.
While even my rarest flaws were borne in demur,
Not a single act of solicitude rested in their core.
While respect was hailed by slaughter,
Every bit of my joy in any admiration was healed to be watered.

While my heartfelt fidelity lay eternally shadowed,
The slightest of deceit forever dazzled.
Where my love and affection awaited recognition,
Mere hatred for petite things appeared heightened.
As if my gratitude towards scholars' help was no vindication,
It was deliberated to be a phony, hiding my condemnation.
And all in the name that *"justice shall prevail!"*
Honesty accounted for nothing,
Decency interminably enslaved.
Where bigger threats than illicit roamed free,
The virtuous man was always caged, buried too deep in the sea.
Although oblivion is common for man to remember the fair deeds of the dead,
Each sin is well versed, at least to criticize the dead.
Though goodness accompanied me to the grave,
Evil ever remained saved... evil ever remained saved!

Bribery v. Loyalty

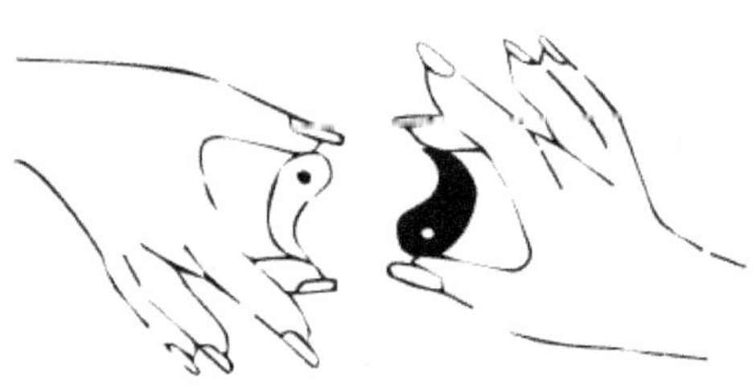

I am a brand, a tradition
A pyramid, a hierarchy;
Favored by the corrupt and unjust,
Unwarranted plus undue officers' oligarchy!
I'm found everywhere,
Under the secretary, over the authority,
Beneath the desk, beyond the rest;
Where sleep lays in dishonesty,
Leaving the nation back with treachery.
Where intellect, solitarily was called success,
And social welfare deserves a disgrace.

Where the country's tomorrow says-
That *"bribe is at the top and complainant at the base!"*
What fame of the nation is left?

When the morrow would obstinately make it
a theft?

But this is what I am,
A new fashion in the contemporaneous
nation,
Of which, even the remarkable feels pride.
I am "*Bribery*",
Known by different names,
Found among most fames,
Have become a system,
And a characteristic trait of the world today!

However, just like every coin has two faces,
I have one too;
The one more deserving than my own.
Lest such emotions prevail where it feels-
"*Where there is power, there lay no virtue,*
But where there is virtue, there is no power!"

I try going towards the virtuous,
But the strong grip of these fraudulent folks,
Clamps and pushes me into their pool of
mischief.

I take risks,
But each time I fall into their evil tricks.
I am poor and have to support,
I'm obligated,
Yet being transitory.
Unlike my contrary,
I'm no coward,
Hiding away from all and lying under the big pockets
I'm brave and stalwart,
Facing the world with fortitude,
With no fear on my head,
And my existence is at the risk of my bread!

This is who I am,
Known by many names,
Somewhere as kindness or decency,
Or integrity
And "*Virtue!*"

So let me not perish in vain,
Let me be at the pinnacle,
And teach the world a lesson!

Hour of Departure

I die watching the limits beyond the sky.
Before the fall, I've touched the high.
These words ought not make anyone cry,
But in my life, I wish they would pry.
What I saw was even beyond the eyes—
Following the limitless, a curiosity to spy
Compelled me, time and again, to question why.
Is it just to live? Yet, I sigh,
To have left my perceptions fall bone-dry.

Life wasn't too short to have taken my time,
To let my ethics dye
Into colours both honest and sly.

There I bid you not goodbye,
But welcome you by this exodus tune,
Which dwindles between both you and I,
Where life eternally holds you by
In the world of a colossal lie.

Sin of Innocence

People may think me to be innocent,
The law may not accuse me of guilt,
But the impending truth hides from none,
As well the impulse knows all my felon,
For it has put me behind bars of miserable
indent;
A path of no return.

Of all the sins known to law are those of
Bodily injury, burglary, arson, and other
contractual flaws.
Heeding not once to gather what
Mental unrest ought to cause.

Indeed, a higher degree of a crime,
A lesser recognized misery

Sparked from distress and agony,
The much needy victim of which
For having made foes with,
Is yet left to fend for oneself.

How emotions have aided to commit
Felonies of greater reach as yonder,
Is no wonder still a whodunnit!

A Hollow Heart

Well I don't understand
Where I had taken the wrong stand.

In the middle of the dark times,
I was awakened underneath the cerise,
Only to realize
I had taken the depraved premise.

None to cater to my misery,
Not a soul to heal the agony,
But all to scream at my catastrophe.

Allegations of a liar,
A scoundrel, and not more than a sinner;

One who worked no more than for mere desire,
I was labelled a felon.

What goes in the mind,
Nobody heeded in the hind
Of a crestfallen, shattered juvenile.
But oft they'd think of
Me a spoiled brat of a rich sire.

For if only people stopped being the judge all the time,
There could be peace
Where man fathoms feelings—
Not the ciphers of coded designs or laws in the charter,
Which people claim to be the language in the banter.

If there be god any,
Must he not have envisioned
A world simple and merry?
Why then chase and hunt a man for man?
Like the prey hunts its ham?

Jail's no punishment to the doer,
Only a burden for the society ahead.
For he is the person
Who cares no more of his own,
Feels no worth for self;
Has no regrets before he leaves,
And nobody's behind to shed tears when he's
deceased.
So, torture is no pain to him,
For he has committed no sin.

None had heard him till he became one,
No one hears him still; he's shut and shunned.
It only boils his blood beyond,
And makes him no less vengeful.
Whips and knives are not fine,
These make cuts alike,
As deep and bright on his spine
As on any other being alive.

Chains and belts are no human curators,
Lest a man goes out of his mind,
The heart may heal it fairly divine.
Hard it is indeed

Even for a surgeon to bring a man back to
life,
Yet not so tough for a diamond
To cut another seamlessly far ajar.

All he wanted was for someone to listen,
Not a cold heart that'd cheat and sear.
For he too, being humankind,
Asked for a love that's loving and benign.

War & Hope

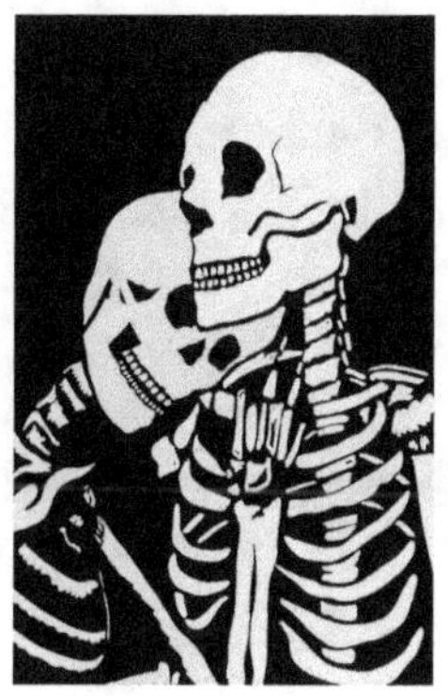

When unrest crept into the hearts and minds
of the world around;
When the bloodshed covered the fields and
meadows
Instead of wheat, barley, and ground;
When the people turned out to be the
butchers of human life;
When chaos between the wrong and right
Seemed far from any sort of fathoming;
When water started to swallow the land from
Earth;
Few stayed, some sighed,
And millions were struck harder than a
bullet,
When the lives of their dears were claimed.

Where edification meant nothing but
assorted ways to kill;
Where not only the human soul was hurt,
But of all those loving hearts and every little
squill.

Then what are you cursing this time for?
Think of the times when the world was at
war.

What do you want more?
Had you been born at the time when the
families were torn,
Would you have had an idea,
How painful it was even to mourn?
Once dead meant forgotten forever.
Buried under the filth
Was the age-old bond that was built.

With the shackles of broken pieces of a frame,
Which once beheld memories of love,
Sits the old woman,
Reminiscent of her man,
"Oh, how beautiful it used to be,

Cried not the the ones who lost,
But those who lived.
When humanity was hit hard,
And cruelty became the principal,
Then was the time when the notes of piano
went off the rhythm.

Say not that you're unlucky,
For they'd been happier with possession of
even a chunk of loaf from a bin.
Repent not that the God's lashing you hard,
For they felt absolved if the bullet hit the
hand, not the heart.

Fight not with thy siblings for softer pillows
on the bed,
For they rejoiced even on finding a brick to
keep their heads up from the earth,
Flooding with blood after the ruckus of
bloodshed.

To sojourn the past

Feels no less petrifying than a memory
Of deceit from mankind.
To those, who lost among the dead,
Their dears,
Only hope and their reason to live,
Now only thrive
To shed tears,
Pitying, what man had made of himself then.
May it revive again to delimit even the most
atrocious of man's visions.

Under the Weighty Protest!

I have to hide behind the walls of this room,
For this mob has come to rule.
I shed tears alone in this gloom,
As opining is going to wound.
Where comrades have turned goons,
In my mind, only fear blooms.
We went past our demands in loops,
And forgot, in the clatter, that the clamour
was for the boon.
Turned up the heat to rise like plumes,
But, oblivious in our demands for rights,
we've ended up in fumes.
Wanting to end living in the doom,

We directed the sails against the wind
To bring the torn sail into loom.
Defending under unity,
We've buried the views of our pals in the
tomb.
Just so might is right,
Every word of a friend was a burning plight.

Dreary days were yet to come,
For the gripe didn't end with the cruel weight
under the crowd,
As even those not part of the bunch were
labelled dumb.
Voices in the air seemed more likely to numb,
For under democracy, there was a spurring
hum.
I cried with the pillow calling for *'mum'*,
As anxiety was the same as someone pointing
at you with a gun.
To raise your voice seemed of no use,
As the mob shall shoo you off, showing a
thumb.

The first tear-drop rolled down the cheek,

As the news spread that the teachers were
shunned.
Reading those notes in my room
Felt like scriptures from the past,
And with a downpour of tears,
I reminisce about the days of their teachings
that shall last.
How years of experience merely yielded them
this appalling adieu;
Exams were just an excuse for this sobbing
heart to subdue the throbbing past.

'tis a never ending tale to tell,
As the protests still went on,
But my fable had ended
When the teachers left their principals
And left their cocoon!

Desire of the Heart

He says she's sweeter than honey,
The sweetest thing that can't be bought with
money.
That her smile would fill his tummy,
But he would never lose her in the rummy.
He looks at her with a protective gaze,
Shielding her from all the rage.
Cares for her like a dried rose in a page,
But the book had closed in a bygone age.
As old as the tale may have been,
So was his love for his kin.

For he knows she remembers that cute little kiss on her chin,
After they first met when the ice was thin.
Though the summer may pass and autumn arrive,
He'll never get tired of calling her alive.
And their story resonates an immortal's vibe,
For eternity has known her more than even he has thrived!

Then why does the merry old man start to weep?
Was she not the treasure for him to keep?
Or did she know too much that God snatched her when He took a peek?
No! But the saga took a leap!

The love he thought was true,
Was just a desire of the heart,
That burnt in the fire of fallacious rue.
Akin to the monsoon patting the barren soil wet too soon,
His love too was felt on the night of the new moon,

With his love reaching the empty, endless
abyss dark sky,
And not the full moon,
She too was no perfect boon.

With her imperfections, she was sent,
With little precision but beauty cent.
Yet he never denied her or let her on lent.
As he prayed, *"tis a blessing and I thank you my
lord!"* and he bent.
Years passed by when she'd bloom back with
his kiss.
But, she would bloom back with the kiss.
In her ways, like a flower, she'd dizzy,
Yet again, he'd only call her his bliss!

She may be fickle,
But none was as fine a man as him,
As he'd endeavour to love her till the last
ounce of it trickles,
Even when her love for him seemed grim.
The autumn of this love was near,
For she was no more a naive blossom,
As she saw his love crystal clear.

Now, together they grew in this love,
With one holding the other,
Without letting the other shove,
And caring as one together.

Now she knew,
That lush pink on her petal-like cheeks,
Those shiny big black eyes that's deep,
That happy face before him that peeks,
The wavy hair tucked behind her ear that
speaks
The language of love,
Unknown to the rest,
Yet closest to his chest,
Where the place lies
For none other than her;
Where she'd bury her face each time she shies,
As he held her softer than fur!

Now they looked into the eyes,
In concert with the desire of their hearts,
As they beat as one and quash all lies!

Closer as they grew,
Further tried their ages to pull them apart.

Yet their bond was as sharp as a dart,
Piercing through the barrier,
Together they had traversed every path.

For age was just a number in time,
A nonentity before this duo's wrath!
Their love was mightier than a sword,
Which they held firm as one in a chord!

Heart of Another

Take me away from all this,
For all my heart's been traded off,
And all that's left for me is to heal the broken
hearts,
And feel the same agony as them all over
again.
Simmering in my own thoughts,
I wonder, where am I going?
Is it the bruises from my past?
Or am I here to make them start all anew?
For every piece of me
Is exchanged for a gallon drops of tears.
If I were not to belong here,
So weren't these shattered hearts.
Yet where is *'my'* wound to be cured?
Is it the bounty of severed and vexed souls
that are to be served?
Or am I blessed with the elixir of love as well?

I command no faculty to rule,
But I'd keep wishing
"If only a love existed in this rugged world,
I'd have thrived in peace and calm."
Little did I know,
That all this time,
It was all within me;
All the love I sought from another!

The Silent Compass

You write,
I'll read.
You express what you may,
And I shall forever be at your stay.
You sway where your dreams sojourn,
And I shall only ground when you adjourn.
You be the striver,
Deep in dreams of eternity.

Fly high,
Vex not the beast of the sky.
For every feather that's shed,
Shall make another step for your flight in the
great beyond.
Dive deep,

For when I am your elixir,
You ought not feel bereft and weep.
Cut through the waters,
Swim to reach the abyss.

For I am the fire in the ice-cold waters,
That ignites the ardour.
For I am that albatross
That guides the sailor
Through the profusion of lies.
For I am that shield of truth,
That the sword of kindness,
That makes enemies bleed
With guilt, drowning in their ego.

Be the prodigy
That paves the way for every novice as gullible
as yourself.
Be the candle lighting the darkest paths of
rue,
Reaching the farthest of the lost travelers.
Be the bud that grows to spread the fragrant
tranquility.
Be that piece of coal, which carves into the
hardest and the shiniest diamond,

Which captures every ray of hope starting
from the dearth of a grave,
To that of the brightest days.

Let every teardrop drizzle,
Singing dewy petrichor
Over the barren terrain, a melancholic
mizzle;
Stronger than the mist,
But lesser than a shower,
Spreading throughout,
Reaching every den, cranny and plower.

Your speech,
A melody to my ears.
Your memory,
My nostalgia.
Your fear,
Creeps in like terror.
Your gloom,
Is my ultimate doom.
You try,
I flourish.
You cry,
And I perish.

You proceed,
I relish it.

So I say,
You write,
I'll read.
You fly,
I'll cover for the fall.
You dive,
I'll cross all the perilous walls in our way!

A Teacher's Sigh...

I take a glance at the crowded room,
Filled with all sorts of countenances, from nerds to bloom,
But my eyes quest for that same earnest look—
Ready to learn, grasp, and yearn for more;
Though there be again those curious eyes fixed on me;
I find not a single face like thee,
Those eager enough, but as calm and placid as the vast azure sea,
Not avaricious for rank or marks,
Nor fastidious behind the raging competition's shaft,
But copiously avowed never to let a chance slip by,
For learning is never a thing to bid adieu.

I take a sigh,
For never a pupil there was,
As one like him.
Embarked on his worth,
Ensued his path,
But left behind,
An indelible mark.
A trail that a teacher seeks to find,
From face to face, from mind to mind.
For he taught me,
That there lay
An innocent yet far too capable child,
Sitting in the same crowd,
Mixing in the ruckus,
Shuffling with the baloney,
Setting a cypher forth the former,
Patiently waiting to be found;
Of the tutor, heeding every sound.
For me, I still have far to tussle
To solve the puzzle.

I try hard to resist the thought of him for a
moment,

However, any extent of my determination
keeps me a failure,
And when I now enter a classroom,
I feel the same melancholy as in an empty,
detached, forlorn room.

My heart grows meek and sheds the tears I
cannot govern,
But ones I owe him,
As he once filled my chest with pride,
That I can neither shove nor shun.

One who gave me the respect I deserved,
One who etched a memoir of himself on both
my heart and soul,
So well preserved,
As no other could've equaled.

My eyes well up hunting for the same gleam,
I look around for 'the' one,
Which once devised in me,
All my curiosity of what a teacher's regard
truly is,
Yet I find not anywhere,
That 'one' face,

Which now a teacher is left to reminisce,
With a deep sigh.

Whisper of the Moon

Who could've known it better than destiny
alone?
That an ocean of praise awaits,
Even the face which glitters in moonlight
alone?
Neither culture nor talents had shown,
Such brightness as the kindled warmth in her
sweet core;
The charm of a lady with a lovely bond,
More did his comely tone
Than anyone had ever made her feel before.

For she lived in a society
Where people believed more in war, rivalry,
and struggle
Than faith, love, and divinity,

She knew not what trust truly meant.
All she knew was
To see the good in each that she could,
But feared every stray that passed by her.
Let alone her trusting one she'd met on the
web,
However much the person might try,
She'd be scared incessantly.

Yet, one fine day,
On her encounter with a man,
Who, though spiritual in belief,
Stirred within her,
Something that kept her up all night,
With the trust he built and the fidelity he
pledged to abide.

She opened her heart to the moon,
The constant companion she had.
No more did she fear the stray,
When the moon whispered,
*"The goodness is in your heart,
And all that's dark shall be away!"*

Honor his Blood

When the world, we start to adorn,
When the new rays touch the ground,
And the moon comes out to mourn,
Even the darkest hour becomes sound.

The wound of the brutal war hurts no more,
For the darkest hour is just before dawn.
The soldier is back to soothe the hour,
Fighting back to save the lore,
For his name to be written in gold:
"An aga to fend the saga!"
Saga of peace,
A tale of humanity,
A fable of trust,
And a legend of faith and hope!

When his blood graced the ground,
The sacrifice quenched the thirst
Of many parched lands,
Of the dead cemetery,
Of the long gone
Oblivious cherished past,
To reunite the forgotten solidarity.

Should the mob zest forth,
To remember his worth?
If his blood drizzled,
To fuse the flooding crowd,
Can't the masses be strong enough to value
his valor,
All his sacrifice and that honor?

Beyond Brute

Let not the shady days blind your way,
For even the darkest hour is before dawn.
Wait not till you see the rays,
For the trail might be long gone.
Watch your back;
Be wary of the sweet sharp lies,
For they shall stab you in the black,
With no hint of it being sly.
Albeit, you have a friend in me,
Giving you my word in troth.
You may lay your trust in me,
For I shan't be the Brute that slew Caesar in a
spree!

Reverie

It's a distant cry,
A mellow reverb,
All tears, but dry,
Hoping one day it'll all curb.

I fear that one day you shall go,
When all I'd ask is for you to stay,
But watching you at my worst low,
Was all my reason to pray:
*"God, please let this pass slow,
For I dread to see that day!"*

It's the nag at the back of my head,
That's back into play,
Wanting to keep you as close as if wed,

But force did not, in my favour, weigh,
For you slipped by like any other old man
bled.

These voices in my head,
Had let the widow in me weep,
Long before he was dead,
Kept me up from my sleep,
And coloured all my nightmares red.

"Hope and pray is all that's left!"
Is what my younger self would've said,
Until I felt his love not bereft;
A saving grace, my only thread,
Covering all the graves I had dug in the heft.
Now his love is all in this heart, that's bred!